piano • vocal • guitar

closer   the best of sarah mclachlan

ISBN 978-1-4234-6752-6

HAL•LEONARD®
CORPORATION
7777 W. BLUEMOUND RD. P.O. BOX 13819 MILWAUKEE, WI 53213

Visit Hal Leonard Online at
www.halleonard.com

VOX

Words and Music by
SARAH McLACHLAN

Moderately

In ___ the des - ert of ___ my dreams ___ I saw ___ you there, ___
Through your eyes the strains of bat - tle like ___ a brood - ing storm. ___
fall in - to the wa - ter and ___ once more ___ I turn ___ to you, ___

and I'm walk - ing towards ___ the wa - ter steam - ing, bod -
You're up and down these pris - tine vel - vet walls ___ like fo -
and the crowds were stand - ing, star - ing face - less, cut -

- y cold ___ and bare. ___ But your words cut loose ___ the fi -
- cus nev - er forms. ___ My walls are get - ting wid -
- ting off ___ my view ___ to you. They start to limp - ly flail ___

6

THE PATH OF THORNS (TERMS)

Words and Music by
SARAH McLACHLAN

In the terms — of en - dear - ment, in the terms of — the

life _____ that you love. __ In the terms of — the years _____ that pass

you by, in the terms of — the rea - sons _____ why.

Through the years — I've grown to — why. *Guitar solo ad lib.*

Fun - ny, how ___ it seems ___ that all ___ I've tried ___ to do ___

___ seemed to make ___ no dif - fer - ence ___ to

you, at all. ___

Instrumental ad lib.

Repeat ad lib. and Fade

INTO THE FIRE

Words and Music by SARAH McLACHLAN
and PIERRE MARCHAND

Moderately

Moth - er, teach me

to walk _ a - gain. _____

yearn for com - fort.

Oh, _____ free the wa - ter that car - ries me to _____ the sea. _____

18

POSSESSION

Words and Music by
SARAH McLACHLAN

HOLD ON

Words and Music by
SARAH McLACHLAN

CODA

love the light___ that brings___ a smile_____ a - cross_____ your_____

___ face.

Hold on._____ Hold on to your - self, ___

___ for this is gon - na hurt like _____ hell.

GOOD ENOUGH

Words and Music by
SARAH McLACHLAN

and I will be there __ for __ you. I'll show you why __ you're so much more than

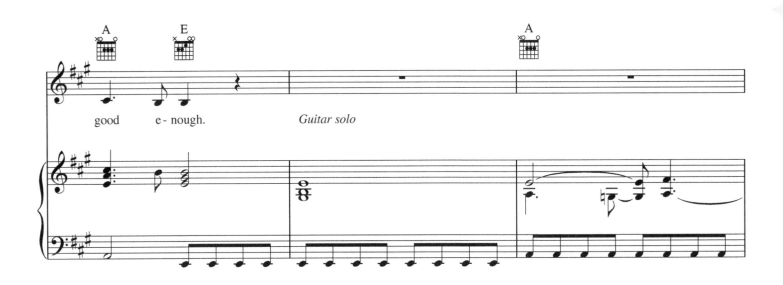

good e - nough. *Guitar solo*

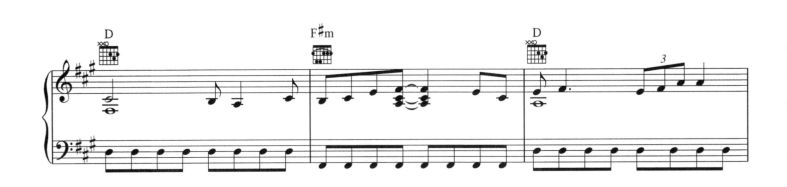

BUILDING A MYSTERY

Words and Music by SARAH McLACHLAN
and PIERRE MARCHAND

ADIA

Words and Music by SARAH McLACHLAN
and PIERRE MARCHAND

Slowly

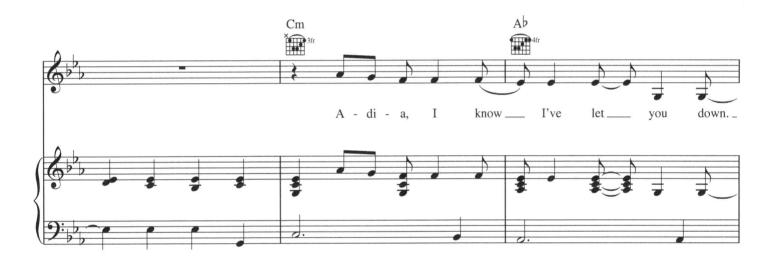

'Cause we are born ___ ___ in - no - cent. ___ Be - lieve ___ me, A - di - a, ___ we are ___ still in - no - cent. ___ ___ It's eas - y, we all fal -

SWEET SURRENDER

Words and Music by
SARAH McLACHLAN

ANGEL

Words and Music by
SARAH McLACHLAN

Recorded a half step higher.

I WILL REMEMBER YOU
Theme from THE BROTHERS McMULLEN

Words and Music by SARAH McLACHLAN,
SEAMUS EGAN and DAVE MERENDA

Moderately slow

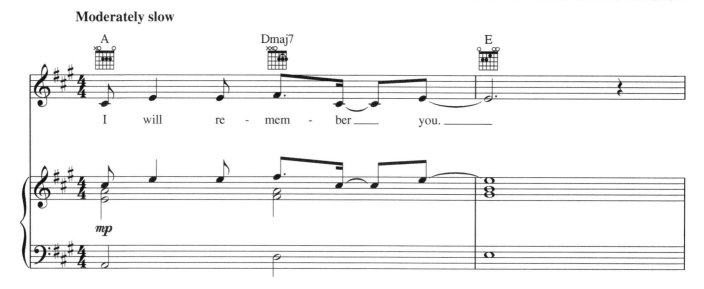

I will re-mem-ber ___ you. ___

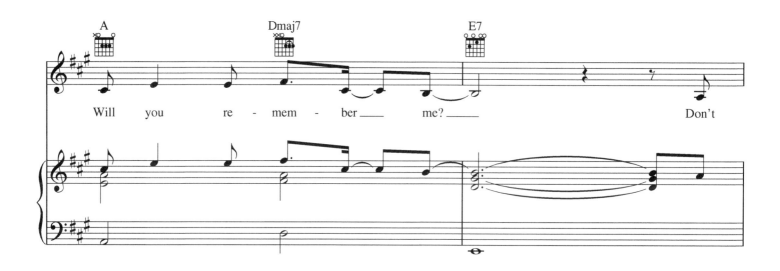

Will you re-mem-ber ___ me? ___ Don't

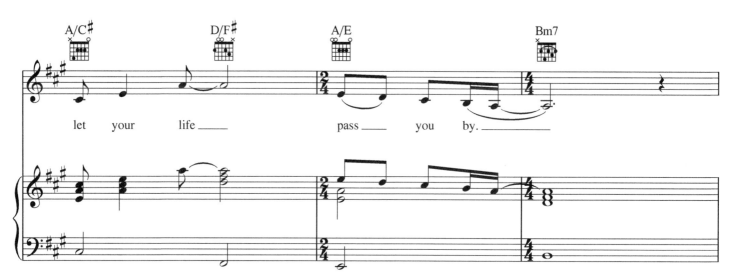

let your life ___ pass ___ you by. ___

STUPID

Words and Music by
SARAH McLACHLAN

Lyrics:

Night, lift up the shades, let in the brilliant light of morning. But steady there now, for I am weak and starving for

Love's made me a fool. It set me on fire and watched as I floundered unable to speak, except to cry out and wait for your

be! A sim - ple - ton could see that you're no good for

me, ___ but you're the on - ly one I see. ___

How stu - pid could I ___

FALLEN

Words and Music by
SARAH McLACHLAN

Moderately slow

Heav-en, bend to take my hand and lead me through the fire. Be the
Heav-en, bend to take my hand, I've no-where left to turn. I'm

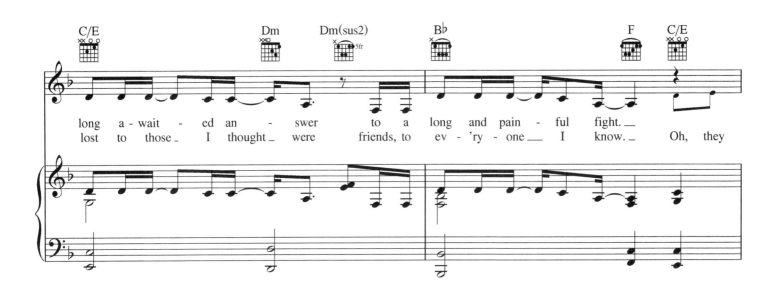

long a-wait-ed an-swer to a long and pain-ful fight. Oh, they
lost to those I thought were friends, to ev-'ry-one I know. Oh, they

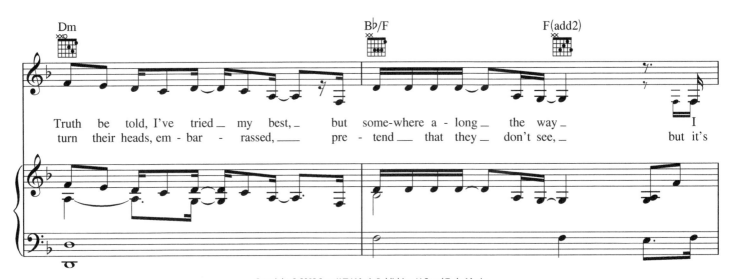

Truth be told, I've tried my best, but some-where a-long the way I
turn their heads, em-bar-rassed, pre-tend that they don't see, but it's

Gm   Bb   F   Csus   **To Coda** ⊕

so don't come 'round here and tell me I told you so.

G7   Bb   A7#5

We

Dm   Bb   F/C

all be-gin with good in-tent. Love was raw and young. We be-

C   Dm   Bb   F   C/E

lieved that we could change our-selves, the past can be un-done. But we

WORLD ON FIRE

Words and Music by SARAH McLACHLAN
and PIERRE MARCHAND

Relaxed groove

Hearts — are worn — in these — dark a - ges.
I watch the heav - ens for my fi - nal call - ing.

You're not — a - lone — in this
Some - thing I can do — to

less we be-come. The for-tune of one ___ man means less for some.

The

DON'T GIVE UP ON US

Words and Music by SARAH McLACHLAN
and PIERRE MARCHAND

Moderately, with a shuffle

Love has __ tak-en me for a fool, __

got-ten out in time __ to save him-self, __ mmm. __

Should have known __ bet-ter __ but I __ let things slide. __ I

U WANT ME 2

Words and Music by SARAH McLACHLAN
and PIERRE MARCHAND

* Recorded a half step lower.